Human Me

Louis Glazzard

Human Men

Illustration by Caitlin McLoughlin
Book design and cover by Caitlin McLoughlin
caitlinmcloughlin.co.uk

Edited by Daunish Negargar

Louis Glazzard
Apartment 217, 5 Blantyre Street, CityGate 3
5 Blantyre Street,
Manchester

louisrowanglazzard.com

ISBN 978-1-5272-9823-1

Printed in the United Kingdom by Pureprint
First printed 09/2021

Contents

Part III

Compromise

Part IV

Men Through the Lens

I started writing Human Men when I first began my journey into online dating. The almost-relationships, the superficiality of dating apps and the vibrancy of gay hook up culture sparked an intense need to process these things through my writing. I wanted to document what makes us human.

I begin the story in the first part of my life where my father was perhaps the worst example of what a parent can be. Violent, an alcoholic and manipulative. I thought I got away unscathed from the trauma of having a parent like this, but in writing this collection many wounds were re-opened. I wanted to ask myself if my fear of men started with my father or with the bullying I received at school for being queer. Perhaps it could be both. I wondered if these were my only Lessons on Men. How could it be that men scared me and yet I am afforded the privilege of being one? How do I love a man if I carry trauma from masculinity?

When I started interacting with men, when I started loving men, the feelings I had about growing up a bullied queer and having an abusive father were an open wound, I'd plastered up under the pretence of thinking I was an exemption. But trauma does not lessen by wishing it away, it exists as you weave through life. It is the second darker part of you that puts on a show in the ugliest of situations. The poems in Human Men and Compromise are situations where I had given into that darker part, but also situations where I'd tried to fight it.

I do not believe now that all men carry some inherent disruption within them. I make generalisations only to offer a perspective found from navigating relationships with them in my life and through my phone. I've found this perspective not just in me, but the people around me too. There are deeper problems I know now that cause this. Society puts pressure on men to behave a certain way. We get aggressive rather than cry. We're expected to keep it in. When you get men like this pushing together for sex and for love it can sometimes become destructive, and, to use an overly quoted word, toxic. These things seem even more accentuated and potent when they are projected through our phones.

8

The story ends in Men Through the Lens by exploring directly, exactly how I've found that technology has mutated toxic masculinity. It also tells a story of me looking for a partner who would have the best traits, exactly what I think it means to be human; loving, emotional and honest. Eventually I did find him, in the strangest and most unexpected of places, which you'll discover at the end of this collection. He supports me in every way I could imagine. He still sits beside me now, knitting and daydreaming, quite so peacefully blowing off the dust I've carried around with me. His love represents an entirely new definition of what it means to love men.

My mother starts and closes this collection because she played an inherent role in shaping these perspectives. As I meandered through experiences, my mother was my protector, advice giver, parent and friend. Her perspectives on these situations and on life continue to shape me and without her, I would not be so equipped to look at these situations with the wisdom and sense of peace I do now.

With all of this, I hope none of us carry around some of the traits we associate with toxic masculinity, because as you might discover in these pages, they can lead to tricky situations. It still bothers me that at points in my life I let myself become toxic. As I've grown I've pushed away from the 'if you can't beat them, join them' plan and instead I search for something new. To write like this means I ceaselessly break the load down. Thank you for carrying this story with me - for letting me discover how to become a human man.

Part 1

Lessons on Men

'In this time of weakness and depression he would have made it his medicine and support, his comforter, his recreation, and his friend, – and thereby sunk deeper and deeper – and bound himself down for ever in the bathos whereinto he had fallen.' - Anne Bronte, *The Tenant of Wildfell Hall*

Mother Dearest

Raised me on Kate Bush
or Bjork boasting
out of weak speakers.

We would dance to it
close together and
I would brush her hair.

The days never end
with your mother
or your first best friend.

Blonde Boy

At the beginning age,
felt a new kind of strange
knowing you were showering
naked in the next room.

My earliest memory -
finding my stomach fuzzy
because of the way your soft cheeks
shivered when you spoke my name.

Rode a bike one village over
because I was your best fat boy.
That night you pulled your penis between
your legs to look like a schoolgirl.

The next day, when I held my first hand
in the cow field behind the town fair,
I couldn't tell my new-bearded girlfriend -
the truths of me wanting you there.

Here, the features of your face sat
in the oval of the burnt-out tire whilst I waited
to feel her. Instead, got scared, you skipped
on my brain - golden hair and lonely name.

The Man My Mother Married

I take you to the breaking point
in a half empty home
with old computer parts
mouldy fridge food and
a cat struggling without its litter
and no space to move.

Here the shouts would befall me
for studying hard. The 'puff boy'
'thinking he's better than me boy'
deployed as reckless weapons.

It took until heads hung over sinks
hair bleach blonde and dangling
our father's pen knife to the deep
line of the wrist and the bullies
with clumps of hair in their hands
to realise
his Bramwell mouth
had emptied out lies.

I became Helen Huntingdon
with my worn out clothes
scribbled on books
pushed into wooden boxes.

My mother grinned
seeing the teenage parts of me in her bedrooms
together we cooked dinner
watched evening television
making new habits
traditions spitting at -
making light of the months of turmoil
and the past.

I sat between my youth and my mother.
We became how we were again
like best friends rekindling,
after hard distractions
and custody battles.

My mother - the protection spell.
The final sanctuary and exit plan
to escape from Arthur
or my drunkard father.

Gaga Shrine

From a booklet
of the star I'd ripped
pieces of her body/aura,
making them bloom,
perform together
on my preteen wall.

Tapestry in her name,
worshipping -
cross referencing
monstrous fame
as a teething path
to my own wound.

Oo-la-la

My father didn't take me
to the dentist because
he was distracted by a feast.

So it was surgery at fifteen
my mouth open like a chasm -
decaying, sugar-filled.

They turned the gas up
too high and I hummed out
my favourite hit at the time.

'Bad Romance' the girl prodding
in my mouth recognised it
so I carried on regardless

singing whilst being probed
but in another world -
high on the pop art of it.

Pizza Buffet

When you're a heavy child
you pursue the fragile comforts.
We find ease in culinary arts -
mouths agape for mozzarella cheese.

Like me, I enjoyed manipulating
my social worker for a full belly
at the buffet, feeding on fries
and thick pizza oiled to its crust.

With mayonnaise dribbling
down my oblivious chin,
and sipping fizzy drink refills
I told her I wanted to stay.

Years pass, my mother tells me
how the stranger had to
apologise and beg in court
for the poorly informed binge.

My mother held a vendetta
but between bites, a simpler me,
was only focused on the letters
of the dessert menu on the table.

My Body as a Mouth

Were you taught to savour?
I was taught to survive
because the next meal
might not come.

I ate food until
my stomach ached
because I was never
taught its language.

Closet

Spent our years together
isolated in time,
pressing our genders together
between book and vine.

Standing at the edge -
a bridge between two towns,
before friendship was currency
and food our worst enemy.

Then one memorable day,
shoulder bags thrown behind us,
out poured the noise -
Who were we really becoming?

That night our strength held
trickling out the news to Tumblr.
We labelled our urges and
confessed our fantasies.

Whispered to each other,
the words of the 'weird' kids.
A secret nestled between us -
best friends for life.

Rowan

He held in hidden secrets,
looking over there ashamed.
That man's interesting looking
or is there something more?
The deep shadow creeping under his jaw.

Tell your sibling and they are
almost too pleased
your friends in high school
are weak at the knees
to finally speak about his details with you.

Your mother reminds you of
the songs she used to sing
and the dolls she let you bathe.
How she brought together your tiny bones
and crafted softness into your middle name.

Bullies

Words would roll off their tongues
like I was their worst nightmare;
fatty; gayboy; don't dare look at me.

> All this before I knew the meaning
> of the word.   The world.

Teenagers are akin to animals
and I fresh meat, was mauled by
intricacies in insults.

> Where are they now? I wonder.

> Instead of carrying the question around,
> I simply write their empty faces
> into these pages
> and bury their words.

The Only Time

When we were young,
we couldn't understand pain.

The past is a painting.
Wet again is the brush
to pull acrylic backwards –
away from the canvas.

That day was the only time
I remember not fearing
the gay jokes.

For they just stood silent –
old friendships became the thick rope
to bind within the fear.

A teenager pulled something unknown
from the back of her womb
without the taste, too soon.

Sitting across from us in chemistry
she told the class the story
of how her instincts had kicked in like hunger.

In a pool of blood she'd wrapped
it up using her torn up
school uniform as his bedding.

(Trauma shredding)

On her Facebook profile I check
to see how she is doing – yearly.

This story had us burnt -
it's the first time I considered,
that care could be an instinct.

When the baby's funeral came
we stood gawking, confused,
staging a school walkout...

The whole school turned up to
the funeral and even the hard lads
who bullied me were softer that day.

We were children trying to find
a christening in her pain.

Lessons on Men from my Father

He can be seen
in nothing but the war books
he left you behind.

Fanatic episodes of you
finding his dried blood on the page
sitting on the shelves between
the new you and your last name.

It's more common he's around
when the 4AM sun begins to pound,
and here you stare -
into the mirror
drunk and baggy
and see your father's sunken eyes.

Fingering the features,
of your father-flesh
lacking his hard hands.

You remember your own face
waving a stick at his son
amongst a forgotten swamp
of qualifications.

Drunkard with a degree
in biology
complaining of disrespect.

The next time you saw him
he was a stranger,
held deep down
in his childhood town's

embalming studio
with make up for the first time
on his half of your face.

You looked at the ground and felt
your feet finally grip to the floor
because his torment
existed
between the breaking
no more.

Your father was the first man
to teach you this lesson - to love a man
is to be an archeologist of pain.

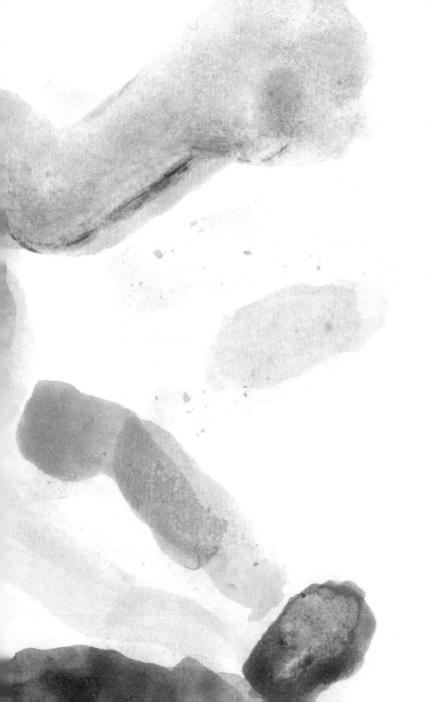

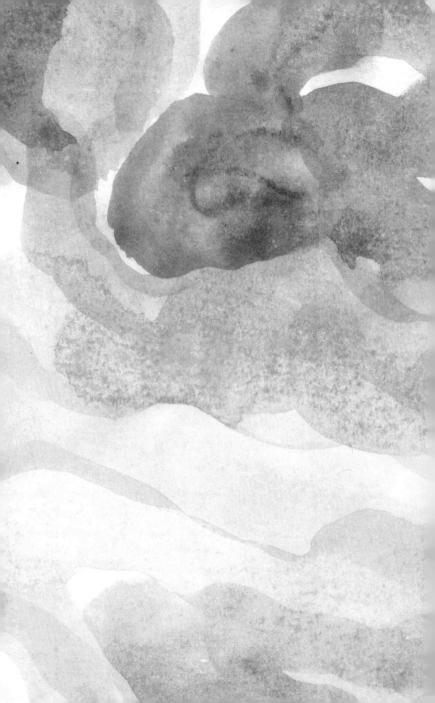

Her Lessons

You stand
on the platform
with coffee cup in hand
looking down at the tracks
whisper now your mantra
to hold up the itching spine in your back.

Dazed, the people stir as
you meander through the train
make your new commute
but you remember her name…

for even before the news
the 'when is she due'
your mother was crafting
artistry through birth
bringing together your bones
and making you
with her morals and rules.

Homeless

My father was homeless towards the end of his life.
The kids at high school told me he was sleeping on market stalls.

The last time I saw my father he threatened to hit me.

My father was the quiet waste of the punk underbelly of England.
Almost the beatnik but never quite hitting it, instead a small
destruction.

The last time I saw my father he was drunk and high on
amphetamines.

My father was full of intoxicating ideas and music collections,
longer than
his arms wailing, fag lit up to Mr Brightside (or something equally,
thoughtlessly provoking).

The last time I saw my father he tried to relate philosophy to my
life.

My father was attentive to the wrong ideals to sickly films where
they travel around homeless and drink until guts empty out.

The last time I saw my father he bequeathed 'Fear and Loathing in
Las Vegas' to me.

He would obsess over the women's bodies in 'The Wicker Man'
pressed up to walls
blatantly glamorising perversion as something to work towards.

The last time I saw my father he was my first angry homophobe.

My father was loving in strange ways which whispered out
between things he'd say
like "I'm proud" once a year before crying like a confused child.

The last time I saw my father he told me you can only go up from rock bottom.

My Father was without conviction but felt loudly crippled by a Thachtered system
so stark were the memories he found no help in change and the intricacies of life.

The next time I see my father it is in the face of every homeless man.

Part II
Human Men

'This more human love (consummated with endless consideration and gentleness, and good and distinct in the coming together and separating) will resemble the one that we are preparing arduously and laboriously' - Rainer Maria Rilke, *Letters to a Young Poet*

Cherry POP

New tradition pulled out of him,
in the hot shower stinging the skin.

At a ripening sickly sixteen
with broken fingernails.

The instigator of magic -
spiders crawled out of your smell.

'Hello Earth' he thought,
falling mottled outside.

Mud stuck to the palms,
just a few steps from home.

I switch narratives, facing a new crux
unbound by the blood stained books.

'What a terrible and bellowing,
belly rumbling night.'

They say the first time should be…
with you writhing around on top of him,

it became a new strange stain.
Let's try and remember his name.

Preparing My Body Fibre

I started working in a gay bar
when I clung to a polite seventeen.

I lacked the comprehension
of some invisible currency.

All the men only seemed
to want to touch my body parts.

Do You Remember this Man?

…that ache… pouring from your mouth
with so much of you begging
to feel.

I remember him you think.
He was _____ ,
had abs to die for and
other important shades,
(features)
that you patch together
in want of a memory.

You trace him back to a best friend
and a premature knot
in your stomach.

When you were older,
with him inside you
in a toilet cubicle
your head pushed down and
you moaning his sweet name
- was this a fantasy coming true?

You felt important right?
…Until the morning
and the mourning -

All the sounds of betrayal
leave tears in your eyes.
All men have legs,
stomachs and absent spines.

Men are men right?

That's when you realised…

You promised yourself
this would be your last
but it could only ever be
your first time.

Grief

You should know this, boy not yet a human man,
this is how those accidents happen…
it's colder with the blinds open.

Here he is, something similar this way comes.
The man that does everything in halves
between your bed sheets and your iCloud.

And yet men are always half pleased,
between pants they whisper it's time to leave,
so here lies the deceit

twitch with your receipt onto tea stained coasters
half made bicycles and rum sweat, deeply trodden,
in a wardrobe of rotten fedoras.

That's where the men coming home with you
are translated and hung up
as a photograph at their gallery display.

Scouting

You appear
under a glassy room.
The mirror reflects your face
open and unrelenting.
A darkness fades into this light -
the morning with no possessions
but only the bare skin on you.

You drank too much last night.
You discover your head is heavy.

There's a stranger breathing
next to you
and a trail of your clothes
towards the door.

Your underwear
lost last
on it goes,
falling back on your body.

The path followed:
in the hallway hollow
now the shirt
on backwards like you left
your own trail to scout out
and your jacket hangs
like a weeping mother on the door.

You're out like a flash
gone in the morning
but pulsing last night
and ending now

at the door frame.
Then to the opening
the buildings become
your beacon
the becoming
beckoning for home.

This is your first time
discovering this strangeness
you walk, directionless but bound
by memory
your own compass
forming.

Later when you wake
to that same confusion
with no memory -
you've been here before.

This was life's orientation
formation
a map, deeply rooted in
the experience of time
raw and endless
unholy and sex-filled.

You lost your mobile phone.
You lost all of your money.
But you found yourself resourceful.

Speaking to my Flesh in the Gym

You breathed out
the fat on your thick thighs
and stopped eating fries.

Here, you became an effigy
turning the wheels
of your mind
combined with the wheels
at the spinning class
toning that
millennial mass.

Paid ten pound for the ritual
daily
to sit at the stool
and have brunch in a bowl
and an almond milk latte.
Making moments

just for your waist
to be skinnier in the club,
making exceptions for
no strings with love
look above
and breathe in the contradiction.

Gloryhole

Part I - Adam

On the first rainy day you were pen ready
to write your usual deflated diary entry -
holding up the flag over orgasming bodies.

Today, here, the sky opened instead
over the twisting. Skin to skin -
he saw your saintly face and fell.

First love seemed brighter than the hips
pressing together, and the violence
dripped out through the brickwork.

Part II - The Fall of Steve

After hearing this godless gossip
a year of peace was lost,
and the anger was inflicted
on your cheekbone.

You begged under the willow tree
by a haunted hyacinth,
Adam punched - you heathen hard
until it hurt the heavens less.

He wept to the angel sisters,
felt hell chafing his fingers
for every time he touched you
your ancient lie lingered.

Adam held an infidelity over you
for one long year of sweeping,
until he found it too sad -
this orchestral weeping.

Part III - Genesis

Years of disciple fucking under his belt
he saw Steve's father voiceless
and selling hats at the Abbey.

He wanted to scream
to the new saint by his side,
But they expect Adam to have no history.

He goes home and finds the old letters
and somewhere he marries you three times
finally forgiving you for your sins.

In anger he sentenced you
to the watering of the dead garden eternal
but even now his stomach sinks

and unwinds when he sees your awe
inspiringly awful
name online.

Or Taylor Swift in Form

Holding your hand limp,
reaching for the bed, I waved
you away from sleeping next to me,
awake all night, you were on the hard floor.

We sobbed when I held your hand
in an all so serious series
of attempts to savour
the sweet taste of our early heartache.

We saved nothing but fear
of the lonely open world.
I felt guilty for a year of reeling you in
to nothing but sickly revenge.

Taylor Swift was me -
revenge song in real life,
embodying her in bedrooms.

Perhaps darling boy, you deserved it.

Final Letter

Dearest first love,

I find myself feeling dizzy/ when the smell of you
on a stranger reminds me. As lovers we made enemies together
breathed in the thick city air/ same sticky throat.
We met for coffee in the old haunt/ talked on things -
the hard habits of our fathers that emptied our stomachs.

Last night, I found myself at one of my many cupboards/
breathless between words of love letters. My hand levitated
them over the shredder - its mouth open. How I begged for
our speedy ending but stalled here. I was a coward to our
memories written out.

In the letter your voice comes back and tells me I stopped you
taking three sugars in your coffee. Now you're gone, my teeth feel
heavier in my jaw. 'Grow old together' I read a final time, and shred
it quick/ mouth aloft with glee.

Sincerely,

growing myself a new spine - guilt free.

Checklist on Heartbreak

Fanning myself with Sarah Kane's plays
crazed on the Subway back down into
Friedrichstien and cheese fries.

The way the man lied to me,
showed his younger photos online,
I was all humour when you implied;

My Fanny Price face is fading
and the pastry man in Prague,
left a mark I thought to be skin cancer.

Instead it was his laughter,
his thoughts on Margaret Thatcher.
My tanned skin lasted in England after

Parisian apartments, and the lack of shame.
"Your beauty isn't quite conveyed online" -
 darling I'm just a product of my time.

Paintings amused by the light, the lure,
of men in leather, ignorance together -
with my darkest fantasies.

Morning leaves in the bathroom. I've found a bin bag
full of middle-aged men's running shoes.
Is the best honesty found in fucking
men twice your own age?

On a bench in Budapest
one psychosis is written,
and one imagined new.

Therapy

The prescription landed in the puddle
and now it's drowned.
With your sleepy tongue you say;
'Do you ever learn?'

Walked down corridors distressed
told you between backpacking
tales of a thousand lovers
and how each had undressed.

Even with yellowing hands,
sunburn on cheeks,
you tell him the weakness
of the person in the mirror is imagined.

Nurture

At the foot of the pine
by the river brewing
emotions whipped up quick
by the stream
trickling between
the leaning trees.

As you and her talked over a man leaving
whistles and breezes
springtime sneezes –
she stays,
listens to you.

In a time of crisis
as the pollen pours out
so does the epiphany
she has always been
the gift, the unwrapping present...

with her words she weaves
an uneven but clear
route to recovery.

Confessional

The way men work brings you to the table together, quoting their lies and worrying about the size of your thighs. In the café today it's a union, a friendship blooming that all makes sense through the pretence of the piece of cake, or the two of you trying to understand them together.

You spent a year together counting calories and a year together in work, a year together nail biting and a year together cursed.

On the phone yesterday you questioned whether you were both the problem but then settled on it being men because then you become sisters under the blister

of the pain men bring to your soft chests.

Waking the Human

Roused by the wind   a brittle plastic
you can smell me.

Bodies and gentle hands
by the worms   mud dreary

I wriggle with it.

Part III

Compromise

'A man comes into my life, and I have to compromise? You must think about that one again. (laughing hysterically)' - Eartha Kitt or my mother

I paid your bus fare...

at the bottom of Canal Street
at 4.15 AM.

'My parents will be home'
you said so I couldn't
spend too long undressing.

The flat cap
hiding your face
was an eternity
of my grandfathers
but the moustache
a story I couldn't
quite locate.

With your arm
clamped over me
I felt I was being
taken into the
mouth of our antiquities

but like any distraction
there are breaks
like the softness
of your hands
not laboured
but moisturised.

I wasn't certain
of why you
traced your tender finger
under my jawline
where my teeth clenched

like you were saving me.
You walked me to the door
of the bus, we hadn't kissed
yet and then I said
'It's too late'
like I'd see you next time
but in the sublime
lesson of the night
you leaned in
'Can you pay my fare please'
so I threw it like a taunted child
at the driver
and walked hunched
into the lighted
heavy blue
and the slew of the city
without a prize worth the labour -
I did not get your phone number.

Tracing Back

Here's hoping time reworked your trauma.
For it has not remoulded your facial expressions
that floated in the darkness of my window.

Your teeth gritted, unravelling in the sheets.
You told me I was an answer for you
but we'd collided at the wrong time.

Here's hoping time has cured your phone addiction
For I worry mine has gotten ever worse,
a pattern I cannot iron out.

I told you to leave if there was to be an extendable
charger separating our naked bodies. Its presence
cold against the skin and you, so thin and shaky.

Here's hoping time restitched your hands
and the ribs weaving together like cloth.
For you told me I wanted too much honesty.

I imagine the marks healing on you now
and so we both remain forever weak
for opening our trousers together, and not our mouths.

Mummy's Boy

I discover too many men
quaking in the evenings
because of their fathers.

I endlessly fixate on my own.

The crack that the mother then fills -
this is a deeper endeavour.

She is open-armed and waiting
a cure for this enduring wound.

Searching for compromise -
I told her and she quipped
back about the insignificance of men.

Good for one thing, I suppose,
these words an answer

to some secrets not yet learned
waiting on the back of my tongue,
crawling limbless through
my begging body.

Before the Conditions Came

Returning to a house of empty bedrooms
after dark streets
and two men holding each other up
arm in arm.   It's 3AM.

The thought of you
pitying my dry skin
will sink me into sleep.

I watched you tonight   male on male
trying to connect   your eyes
with my drifting mind
the thing pulsing between your thighs.

An unwelcome couples portrait
still saved in my phone.
A giggle   a pant
                    a political rant
and a final screaming out of some pain,
I think we'd both whispered.

My skin usually cold, has felt belonging
despite this being
a 'not too serious' thing
only two weeks old.

Family Habits Die Hard

On the bench under the apple tree
my grandmother tells me
about her husband and rubs
the ring on her finger, searching…

In the evening I ache over my ancestors.

A narrative becomes mine -
I open my grandmothers mouth
by the window   smoking
not worrying enough
about the family curse.

Unfortunate Fortune

Sitting in your exhibition
a woman read my fortune
told me 'love' was around the corner...
You collected your things to go -
scared of the word.

Art Boys (Barbican)

At the art gallery,
when you kissed him
in the elevator, upward
to the city views
he found you
his next muse.

This city is painted,
plastered with faces.
For a town so small
he has made love to all
of the men you imagine.

You left the walls peeling,
red stained eyes show
the imprint, trace paint
with your soft finger,
and think how you crafted him -
as a stain on your next city.

Where sickness sits,
on your stomach,
on the canvas
a pattern that dries.
Remember he came to you
without their familiar lies.

Hanging in the gallery display
remember when you heard
his dry lips say
'Together we were absurd.'

A masterpiece experienced
through glass is always blurred.

Nail Biting by South Friars Bay
/ with Conditions

Shipwrecked, South Friars Bay
my mother takes us away
to reward an all clear.

The boy is the way
the sun looks with its
head eclipsed by the moon,
tipped to the side too soon
and then comes the darkness –
every part of the day leaving.

I entertain myself –
watching the waves
fighting soft knuckled
to see who can reach
the furthest up the beach.

The orange lights on the bay
made me text: 'I may
miss you'.

I crushed my palm into the sand,
reminding myself
you don't like it
when your men bite their nails.

When my nails sting –
breaststroke in the sea.
Were you doing a favour,
changing bad habits in me?

Presence

In the heat of the bar underneath the sun
she points out a beer and mutters
'It reminds me of your father.'

Symbiotic are the sky and her bosom
clear of the uncalm. See the opening
of the clouds and hear the syllables sing.

Loving a Man with Terms and Conditions

...never did run smooth.
The clock has hands
and I trapped them for you
sun up; words read,
malfunctioning
over the phone.

There was a man
in between me and you
and he's still around,
when I notice I have been
folding my clothes more.

Whilst folding I think
I've run out of shirts
to impress you with.
I'll have to buy more.

Picture in a frame
stomach upset,
I'll send my arms to you
in the mail
but I don't know if they'll arrive
before Sunday.

A month later
I know you as 'Time to go'
always saying five more minutes
at the ticket stall
4:02pm with last nights wine
in my bitten fingernail,
I had a little heartburn.

Your invite to dinner
rescinded in a text
disturbed me less,
than it could have
if only I still knew you
as I knew you yesterday.

Bloodstain

Laid out with crabfish, Mother had crafted a plan
with the delicious ticking of the bathroom fan.

On the boat basking and by Frigate bay
there were lessons unravelling, words to say.

A history in both of us learned,
that wide armed part of me still yearned...

for my father and his grubby penknives
but lo! - mother's truth is rising with the tide.

Bath Bomb

Two boys
drift together
entwined.
When you pulse
next to me
I feel the way
the lighthouse feels
when it kisses its light
reflecting on the sea.
In the bedding you sink
in and out of me.

Dripping into you or your bath,
the lighthouse behind us,
I thought how I had
never seen someone
look so good naked.
But the bath
became too small
for our egos,
and now the waves fade
we anchor at the bay
harboured in sleep
but we were better at sea.

Becoming my Mother in the Train Station

My mother once told me a story
of how she had wept
at a bus stop
because a man had emptied her.

In the train station,
when it was over with him
I embodied her
a history repeating boundlessly.

A sharp painful inhale
and ten thousand iMessages
Did naught to quell
the rebirth.

The lesson of the many
mothers before mine
left my fingernails cracked
those bitten, cursed reminders.

Final Gifts

Chasing a night closure on the M5,
always wishing you were mine
but we were always itching for time
and it took this boy less than a week
to change his mind.

The bump under tyre,
tap trapping of the keyboard -
time creates our mistakes.

There are types of
boys that make you think
you can't change,
sitting all deranged...

your gift is a month to wait.

I sat at the end of my bed
nightly, waiting for him to pull out
his phone and play a game
of ignoring the message under my name.

Head hangs loose on a line and a lie
'I wasn't looking for anything serious'
or the 'It's different this time'.

At 2.38AM, blurry screen
I got used to feeling
in between something
and nothing with him.

On the few nights
he had actually spared for me
I would lie awake and watch him breathing

the sparkles of the night, my audience,
I whispered out some truths to
the dark air and his sleeping body.

Yet his hair was still upright,
ready.
Teeth locked down for a smile,
teasing.

You shouldn't trust a man who
looks cute sleeping.

You blink, the rest of your coffee
in the sink and it's another morning
he's making you feel alone.

Thoughts on a Medicine

Mixing in
the smell of myself
with a lime
and the smell of milk
on your breath.

Irish mumble
drunken tease
telling me your mind
would be at ease
if you were married.

The contradiction in you
and our sexual ceremony,
I couldn't grasp at it,
as I grabbed you by the neck
and you hymned out;
'Safe word: pomegranate.'

Mother I'm a Mean Boy

O are my schemes up?
O am I done playing games?

Gold and floating
wine glass
your face and I stared into my reflection -
thought of you

Saw a flash of gold hair
peel over my eyes -
thought of you.

Scenes of us in the dark
last night, learning about each other
stopped my itching,
and the aching in the morning
you stood over me
and talked about being tired
of dating men and their excuses.

An old man whispered at my window,
told me it was time to let someone new in
but there has been another man,
silent in my room since you arrived.

Welcome to the next episode
letting out wisdom
over a pub window
on the quayside
epitaphs of affection
in the end credits
to these scenes.

I'm sorry it just felt good
to play the boy being mean.

List

My bones were scrubbed clean
by connecting strangers to you.

You sang 'Running' to me in the sheets
and sprinted a million long miles away.

I obsess over the word 'alone'
and smell jazz on the metro.

Yesterday I wrote a list of 77 reasons
these human men had left me.

Part IV
Men Through the Lens

'Nothing is pure anymore but solitude. It's hard to make sense, feels as if I'm sensing you through a lens.' - Mew, *Comforting Sounds*

'Technology does everything for us so that we no longer have to function in terms of experience. We function in terms of aesthetics' - Jack Goldstein

HTTP CV

Profile:
I slay but
I'm aching inside me. The way the world works.
Why are you reading this?
Look at my Instagram followers
bitch.

Key skills:
• social media
• can read a book
• has enemies
• scaring heterosexuals
• scaring myself by googling my symptoms

Experience:
XXX - to Present
Find me under sheets. It's where we'll meet.
On the app, double tap.
We can make memories together online.
I'm a mentor for myself.

Birth - XXX
I was an artist. But the world told me no.

Interests:
Trash TV
Hangover anxiety
Alternatives to the everyday
honest fucking

Achievements:
Cum stain on my bedroom wall

References available when I digest.

!?

159 matches on Tinder
and I'm still not married.

Men want my body on Grindr
but no conversations are carried.

100 Hookups

Quaking message pings,
replaced authentic flings.
Under the woodwork, the lie online worked
and your phone buzzes in a swarm,
millions of delicate people
at your fingertips - you find…

The Scottish man who wanted to show
you his aged body in a damp tent
on the coast of France
who told you to meet him
down at the beach
the next day for more.

The man who called you a whore
and yet died twice
hearing his girlfriend come home or
the door to his apartment go
−scrambling for your purse and plans
leaving the reception lobby flustered and

The man who held up his paintings
in the attic room, almost fainting
through the drugs he had fed you
like a bottle to a baby's mouth
but all of this felt new
an excitement until...

You saw your future in the man
who made love to you against
a cold window over the city
before you spent the next morning
between the pigeons and the pills,
his '100 times' had you breathless at the clinic.

In the mornings your mother
was waving at the station
as you emptied out the truth to her
and decided on breath - out, in,
but now, standing on the platform
you grieve

because...

you will never understand men.

Deception

The young men at 25
who followed you online
found you in your baseball cap
and left you a faded map...

to the shape of the square screen
leaving you wondering
what all of this noise means.

A cocktail with lime
breeds this time
an aching.
Invading flesh,
pink and protruding.

Salt ridden eyes, always your own,
a mud masked stranger lets you
into his home.

Broken door handle
dusty bed lamps
bedroom heavy with damp.

As you leave after making love
dazed
drowsy
and drained
by the social age.

The trail to the foot
of your youth
pulses in your head.

Why did you find a knife,
under your lover's bed?

Instructions I wrote to quell dating app shame

1) Delete the apps ten times in a week because using them is like breaking open a wound
2) Settle on other revenge tactics like selfies
3) Take ten, choose one
4) Stretch your chin thin with your finger - photo edit
5) Post and wait for messages - hedonism personified
6) Feel the wound gape anew but have a reason to feel pretty

Weaponising Social Media

Double tap...

                  all of these men have similarities
                  I see them lined up, aiming at me,
                  feet sinking in the field of mud
                  on my dry lips, linger the deadly words...

Under my pillow
Lo! His mood is low
What's in the silence?
the place men go?

                  Wait for the chasm to open -
                  Will it be legs or siren mouth?

Selfie, masc queen, 2:40AM

Oh word up, type it, I know how
to make men miss me
want me. Hold up, hang on
post that selfie darling
you look somewhat sickening.

Sicken them yes, to their stomachs
when they see me pulsing
and mimicking worth,
muscle and beard
performance art, pausing.

Did you forget to pursue me?
Well this will make you remember
I cackle and think all you men
you're dogs, need training.
I am starting to hate men
because our fathers made us hate them.
Never again will I let new romance
even out my edges, leave me choking
instead you have to be the one chuckling.

I have been the nail
and I'm striving, starving
begging for some way
to be the hammer
even if it means showing my body
to strangers. Class goes out the window
when you're a widow
of a half empty kind of love.

It's the end of the day,
the nervous twitching hasn't gone away
so I put my black and white body on display.

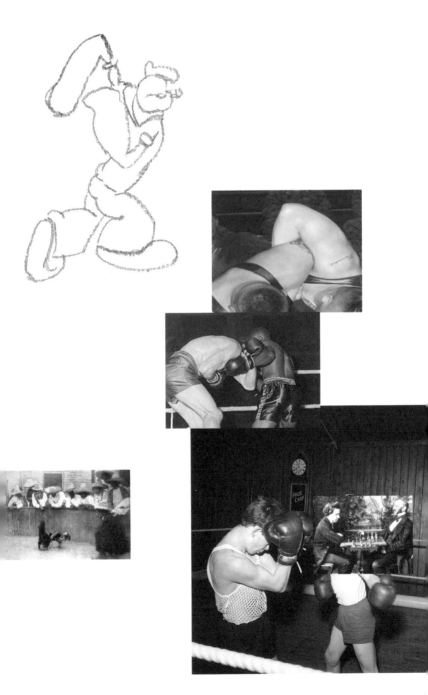

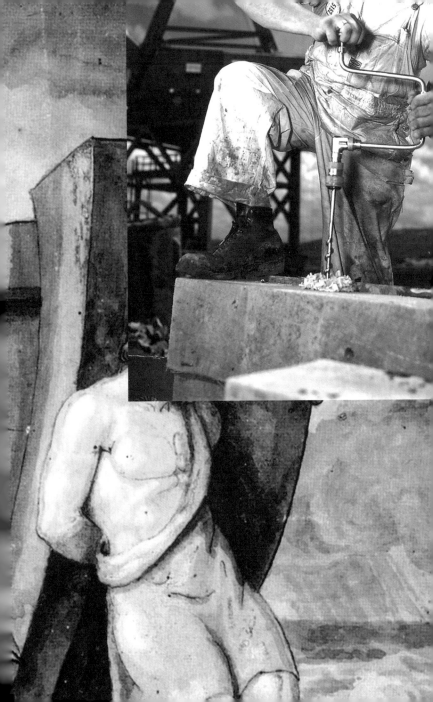

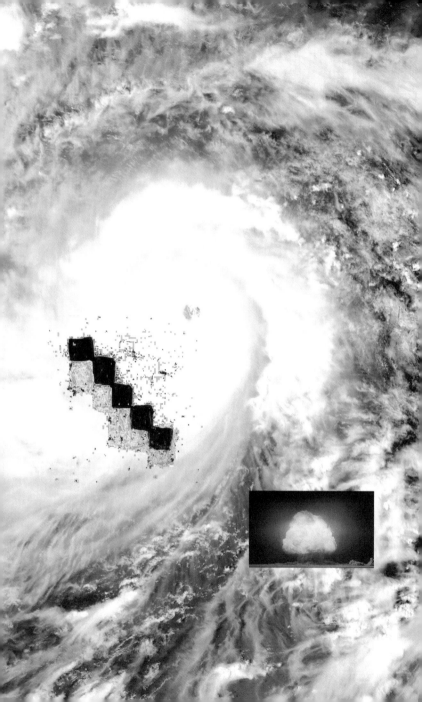

Read: 8:24

There was a silence between you and him
knotting you into his sheets
as he stroked the patch of dry skin
under your knee.
The hair on his legs stood to attention
like guards to battle.
He asked you; 'Do you have bed bugs?'

There was a breathing between you and him
in the bed less lumpy than yours.
Last night his neighbours vomited
into his garden.
You twisted your foot to the smell,
the ankle clicked
and it felt familiar.

There was a kissing between you and him
when you tasted on his tongue
the lovers who confused you.
You both commented on it
that you'd shared this in a strange way.
So, then you babbled away until
you felt you had taken a joke too far
when he turned away to sleep.

But then there was a memory between you and him
when his breathing halted,
it expired into a snore
and again, you searched
for a promise in the collage
of scars and hair on his neck
and the way they connect
to his hairline.

There was a cease-fire then between you and him
until he turned over in the morning
his face dry
the fluffy light fitting into
his morning moan.
You traced each other with a fingernail
and told the window
it was invading your weekday.

There was a truce between you and him
when the unbidden noon hurried in
the curtain opened
and he sat slouching up against his pillow
tapping his fingers on the wall
the sound telling you
it was time to start the dangerous thing
they call the day.

There was silence between you and him
when you walked ten minutes home
and you worried over his own worries
enough to need two coffees
to covet your breath
remove this taste
of being left on 'read'.

BLOCKED

Under my skin
some of my bones still ache,
flesh heating through
the thought of you.

So here we meet in hiding
I see in this grey tile
regrets
but old love too,
be with you
in the willingness
to learn to forget.

We stopped for breath
filtered it filled us
the expanse of a field
between us and your fears.

Those inconvenient memories
of me singing in the passenger seat
twisting between each other -
with you always wanting
to chase someone else.

On the nights we struggled
to find each other
my mind leaves my body
as you become
every man I hated to love.

How many lovers crawl from your stomach
and remember your smell?

Lost iMessage

Smelling cheap aftershave
in the department store
your neck crisp and clean
comes back to eclipse my memories
small and insignificant.

Social Media Stalking (SMS)

In our minds, why do we turn over
the men that hated us?
Left us with our stomachs curdling
because of their kisses and why
does their flirting, stripping us,
gut wrenching
leave us winded?

I am slumped over phone reaching,
hearing, the voice of my
(Ex-lover.)

I scroll through time
his year without you   finds you with
no reference
no news…

              they change in little ways.

Truth of the Few

You turned to me, eyes eclipsed
by spectacles, wizard-like.
You told me, a golden prophet
'Who are you are online is…
perhaps never the person
you are in real life'

Imperfect humans pressure

           under

               buckling

                    from the weight

                         of the social world.

Found a Human Man on Instagram

There are spells in the days
we spend in my bedroom -
forget about time.

There is beauty in your features
which fit perfectly on your face -
voice mending me.

There is a future in the list
of films we've typed out together -
the first one crossed off.

Men should never save you
but I forget the other names -
syllables die at the door.

I call you a small boy and think
of you charting with tiny hands -
this new male condition.

We are a masterclass together
teaching each other a way to recover -
lesson title; 'No Terms and Conditions'.

Dating App Requiems

In the village
we walk together
our hand holding here
is controversial,
you say in the mornings
thin lipped   groggy.

We spot a scarecrow bowing
paper mache dragon winding
rustling away into a tree.

You take me home to the bristling
of your childhood bed sheets
and we christen them with our future.

Caught between books   yellowing plants
                    I unbutton your pants.
Underneath them
I trace with my furrowed hands
the home that made you,
paint   peeling
and later   feeling
your body   your blemishes
dirt tracks tracing
your coarse hair.

Between your grins,
and symphonic breath -
I accept this charity.

My socks are yellow
since I stand outside too often,
to hear the birds

and the chimes of a village
listening up towards the molten sky.

Amongst the distractions
the syllables tweeted and
my mobile phone
feeling like an urge –
they never brought me
to this becoming.

My Mother Teaching Me Technology

Laid out   bath fresh
on a rusty   sun lounger
caught between

           a book

             purple cafetiere.
               I'd be there

     but in a different world.

                Tired eyes of hers
        looked up at   Arden trees
                she'd tell me;

    'Get off your phone Louis
        because oh!...
           there are so many
             stories
        we can tell
          ourselves.'

Notes

The work carried out on this book would not have been possible without the help of Arts Council England and the National Lottery which was developed directly because of their funding. Through the grant we were able to write and edit the contents of the book.

Illustration, printing and distribution of the book has been self-funded.

Gratitude to the following places for publishing earlier versions of some of the poems published in this collection:

Man My Mother Married as Now He's Gone (BRAG Writers)
Pizza Buffet in Polari Anthology Nº1: Creating in Crisis (Polari Press, April 2021)
Cherry POP (Queerlings)
Deception as Grindr Gone Wrong (Untitled: Voices)
Bath Bomb (The Waxed Lemon)
Nail Biting by South Friars Bay, Final Gifts and Read 8:24 (New Critique)
Mother I'm a Mean Boy (Nightsweats Zine as part of Gullaume Vadame's solo exhibition celebrating the life and work of Thom Gunn.)
100 Hookups as Tinder vs. Grindr (LGBTQ+ Community Centre in London)
Social Media Stalking (SMS), Weaponising Social Media, Selfie, masc queen, 2,40am as audio/visual pieces (Pride Inside for Waterside Arts and Creative Industries Trafford, May 2020)

Image Credits

Cock Fight Arina, Davao, author Paul Lewin, licensed under CC BY 2.0, cropped **88**

Hooligans Fenerbahçe, author Subutay1000, licensed under C BY-SA 4.0, desaturated **90**

Architect with students at the drawing board, author Zentralbild Gellina, (Bundesarchiv, Bild 183-16229-0001) licensed under CC-BY-SA 3.0 **91**

Plastic chairs at a football stadium broken by hooligans, author Zac Allan, licensed under CC BY 3.0 **92**

Panathinaikos Paok 1989, author George Mirgiannis, licensed under CC BY-SA 4.0, cropped **93**

FDGB Cup, 1. FC Lok Leipzig - Dynamo Schwerin, riots, author Wolfried Pätzold (Bundesarchiv, Bild 183-1990-0414-009), licensed under CC-BY-SA 3.0, cropped **93**

FC Carl Zeiss Jena - FC Berlin, Ausschreitungen, author Jan Peter Kasper, licensed under CC BY-SA 3.0 **93**

Supporters of PSV Eindhoven in Lille, author Liondartois, licensed under CC BY-SA 3.0 **97**

Apollo synthetic diamond, author Steve Jurvetson, licensed under CC BY 2.0, pixelated **101**

With the exception of the images licensed under Creative Commons licenses as stated above, all found images used are taken from the Public Domain.

Acknowledgements

Thank you, Arts Council England and the National Lottery for funding the early stages of this project, giving me the time to write and work with a professional editor.

Daunish Negargar, editor of New Critique and various other published works, performed as an editor for the whole text. He has my endless gratitude for treating my work with care and transforming it.

Caitlin McLoughlin illustrated the work and took this poetry somewhere, visually, I could not have.

I'm proud to call both Daunish and Caitlin collaborators and friends.

I am grateful for my late mother Karen for teaching me literature, for being the best example of what it means to love unconditionally and for being my protector.

I thank my sibling, Hev for constantly healing my wounds, teaching me to believe in my art.

My partner Simon for teaching me a new male condition.

Endless gratitude to my nearest and dearest friends who have had incredible influence in shaping me as a writer and as a human being.

And finally, a thank you to the poets who taught me so much about my writing.

About the Author

Louis Glazzard (He/Him) is a working class queer writer and poet. He was born and raised in Yorkshire, England. Louis' poetry has been published in various journals and magazines and he has previously been awarded an Arts Council National Lottery Project Grant and worked as a BBC New Creative. Louis is now based in Manchester where he lives with his partner Simon.

louisrowanglazzard.com

Follow Louis Glazzard on social media.
Instagram, TikTok and Twitter: @lourowpoet